# NAVIGATING CO-PARENTING WITH A NARCISSIST

# NAVIGATING CO-PARENTING WITH A NARCISSIST

HANLEY STANLEY

# CONTENTS

| | |
|---|---|
| Chapter 1: Introduction | 1 |
| Part I: Understanding Narcissism in Co-Parenting | 3 |
| Part II: Establishing Boundaries with a Narcissist | 7 |
| Part III: Cultivating Peace and Stability in Co-Pa | 11 |
| Part IV: Focusing on Raising Secure Kids | 15 |
| Conclusion | 18 |

Copyright © 2024 by Hanley Stanley
All rights reserved. No part of this book may be reproduced in any manner whatsoever without written permission except in the case of brief quotations embodied in critical articles and reviews.
First Printing, 2024

# Chapter 1: Introduction

Navigating co-parenting with a toxic narcissist is among the most challenging experiences one can face as a parent and an adult. The extreme nature of narcissists—their need for control and manipulation—can turn even the simplest parenting exchanges into a battlefield. Because narcissism is rooted in self-love, it is neither illegal nor typically a primary reason for a court to restrict a parent's time with their children. Consequently, post-divorce, we must learn to build a new life as parallel co-parents with a toxic ex. In this book, I will explore key topics such as keeping yourself safe, building boundaries, finding peace, and raising secure kids despite the co-parent's efforts to disrupt these goals.

As an author, coach, and speaker who has endured a messy co-parenting experience, I frequently encounter individuals navigating their own terrible co-parenting situations. The issues they face are diverse, often including how to share information between homes, protect their children, and rebuild their lives as single parents. Many seek tools to manage their narcissistic ex-partners, aiming to maintain peace or establish stronger boundaries when possible. Ultimately, many parents want to feel more confident in their ability to foster a secure environment for their children.

**Understanding Narcissistic Traits in Co-Parenting**

Have you ever dreamt of your co-parent healing from their personality disorder? Imagining them becoming someone kinder, more curious about you, wiser, and cooperative in caring for your beautiful child? For many, this was the initial hope on their co-parenting journey with a narcissist: that the exile of the narcissist from goodwill, health, and humanity might not be permanent. In our darkest hours, who hasn't wished the universe would spare the children of a narcissist, overflowing with love, in a miraculous cosmic twist? This hope sustains the goodwill you have toward your co-parent.

Family courts share two things with you about co-parenting with a narcissist: first, they also wish for the future goodwill of co-parents. Judges understand that a successful co-parenting relationship benefits everyone, particularly the children. Second, both the court and your goodwill acknowledge the narcissist's tools of seduction are impeccable. They can manipulate your desires with an image of what you wish for, often disarming you too late.

But let's move forward. Let's explore how to discover freedom that doesn't rely on the goodwill of our co-parents. Instead, we can invite their grace, partake in it, and witness, as they are energized by our invitation to passion, their love flowing as parents into our children's lives. This is how genuinely good parents, capable of goodwill, behave.

# Part I: Understanding Narcissism in Co-Parenting

When we talk about co-parenting, it's normal to discuss cooperation and collaboration in parental care. However, it has become increasingly common to discuss co-parenting in the context of a relationship with someone who has narcissistic personality disorder (NPD) or strong narcissistic traits. You may be someone who never recognized active or passive traits of narcissistic personality disorder before co-parenting with one.

It's important to understand that if you're here, you're likely dealing with someone you believe has a personality disorder. The fundamental nature of such a disorder is that those who have it are not troubled by how they treat others and have very little incentive to change. A well-known trait of narcissists is their difficulty with taking personal responsibility for negative outcomes, even when they are largely to blame. They often adopt roles of victim or martyr. Before hoping that their awareness of a problem will lead to change, it must be acknowledged upfront: it is unlikely that your co-parent will change, even if they recognize they have NPD. Reading all the relevant literature will not alter the behavior of a parent with a personality disorder. It will not reduce the trauma of co-parenting with a narcissist or dealing with inexperienced family courts. The key strategy is to design a parenting plan that rests on more normative shared values included in a court order, rather than the details of a high-conflict parenting plan or policy book that restricts co-parenting. This approach can help contain the chaotic and troubling trajectory of the ex-partner with narcissistic personality disorder.

**Defining Narcissistic Personality Disorder**

A narcissist is not just someone who is arrogant or self-absorbed, but also emotionally unfit. Narcissistic injury occurs when someone confronts them with the truth and rejects their facade, hence the term "narcissistic injury." The term "narcissist" is used to describe someone with Narcissistic Personality Disorder (NPD). NPD is a medically diagnosable personality disorder that affects the way a person thinks and feels about themselves and others. While some people may exhibit symptoms of narcissism, only around 1% of the population will meet the full criteria for the diagnosis.

A person with NPD can display grandiosity, behaving as if they are above everyone else and only associating with others whom they deem similar to themselves. Narcissism can also include misogyny and discrimination. The intensity and consequences of one person's narcissism will differ from another's, but it primarily involves NPD. Even when you point out these biases, narcissists engage in intrusive activities such as defamation. Although cognitive-behavioral therapy can help people with various personality disorders, managing narcissism, specifically NPD, is challenging. However, treatments are available. To accurately identify the characteristics and actions of a narcissist and craft strategies to minimize the likelihood of further harm from their vulnerable rage, it is crucial to sharpen the skills of survivors.

**Impact of Narcissism on Co-Parenting Relationships**

Understanding how to navigate co-parenting with a narcissist requires looking at the specific traits that make it different and how it impacts children and the co-parenting relationship.

1. **Rigid Worldview**: Narcissists generally believe their worldview is the correct and only way. They feel entitled to impose

their vision onto the world and expect others to follow. This often leads to a lack of boundary recognition for the child, who is seen as an extension of the parent. While this can appear loving, as the parent often wants to show off their child, the child is actually unable to express their true self.

2. **Ego Inflation**: Individuals with NPD often need their ego inflated, usually through others feeding their desire for adoration. To "win" the child over, a narcissistic parent may use manipulation and alienation, appearing as the ultimate parent while diminishing the other parent. As the child grows older, the narcissistic parent may brag about the child to show how much better they are than the other parent.

3. **Difficulty with Criticism**: Narcissists struggle with constructive criticism and are quick to blame others when things go wrong in their children's lives, rather than problem-solve and work on solutions. This complicates the already complex task of co-parenting.

4. **Perfectionism and Mistakes**: Narcissists are perfectionistic and usually fail to recognize their own flawed thinking. In divorced situations, splitting and turning children against the other parent is common and can often be addressed with therapeutic interventions. However, when the alienation tactic is used by a narcissistic parent, it becomes nearly impossible to separate the delusion from reality in the eyes of the child.

# Part II: Establishing Boundaries with a Narcissist

## Setting Clear and Firm Boundaries

**Setting clear and firm boundaries** is the first step to effectively co-parenting with a narcissist. Establishing predictable routines is crucial. The person you're working with already has experience navigating their relationship with their kids, so to avoid stepping on toes and causing unnecessary pressure, it's important to learn about the existing schedules and routines of the household. Create a safe environment where the child can develop a routine over time without being exposed to too much change. Engage in fun activities with your stepchildren that foster good memories and cultivate a relationship over time.

When co-parenting with a narcissist hasn't reached a state of peace and acceptance, you're bound to have repeated conflicts. To avoid this, you need to **establish rigidly firm and non-negotiable boundaries** and stick to them. On forums like Chump Lady, you'll find countless stories of people who were bullied into seemingly trivial and nitpicking arguments, from where a child sat on an airplane to what time the child was dropped off or picked up. Such conflicts are designed to cause anxiety and frustration because they serve the narcissist's needs.

Developing boundaries and managing the narcissist's need to "discuss" these boundaries is essential for maintaining peace. As any family law attorney will tell you, **boundaries and clear, unambiguously written orders** are the best tools. Accepting the reality of who your co-parent is and stepping onto the bridge of peace yourself is the only way to create a secure co-parenting environment. This bridge of peace allows you to focus on yourself and your children, shielding you from the chaos and unpredictability of the narcissistic co-parent.

**Enforcing Boundaries Effectively**

Once boundaries are established, enforcing them effectively is crucial. Begin by labeling unwanted behavior quickly and efficiently with direct and honest language, offering minimal to no detail. For instance, if your partner goes on a two-hour verbal rampage in front of the children, calmly suggest a separation with a statement like, "I will find a space to cool off, and we will discuss this in public." During this separation, remove the children from the line of toxic and manipulative behavior, using the time to console and uplift their spirits. After a boundary has been crossed, convey to the children that the behavior was wrong, but avoid discussing the situation further out of respect.

Enforcing boundaries effectively requires a clear understanding of what is reasonable. For example, after a custody hearing, requesting a summary of the evidence presented is a reasonable boundary. However, demanding every grainy picture taken by the other parent to see if your child appeared in the background is not. Boundaries are only effective when they are both reasonable and enforceable.

**Communicating these boundaries effectively** is also key. Establishing a low-conflict communication platform and sticking to it is essential. When communicating a boundary, decide whether to send a one-off message or use a standard response for ongoing issues. A one-off message communicates a specific decision, such as, "It is my turn to tell a story at bedtime. Going forward, please leave her Kindle or any other electronics in your room when it is my turn." This sets a clear time for the child's tech break.

A standard response might look like this: "I understand that you need to put the child to bed on the fourth Sunday of October. I will expect my make-up time per our court order." This informs the other parent of a boundary that will be enforced consistently.

If an effective low-conflict communication strategy has been utilized and the boundary is still crossed, it's time to reevaluate and impose consequences as necessary.

# Part III: Cultivating Peace and Stability in Co-Pa

## Strategies for Managing Conflict

**Peace and stability** are crucial for raising healthy children. However, these terms can be subjective, meaning different things to different people. For the purpose of this guide, peace and stability refer to the attempt to limit, minimize, or productively manage overt conflict through neutralization, which can serve as a protective factor for both co-parents and their children. Conciliatory and positive co-parenting styles are associated with higher levels of security in children. By neutralization, we mean professionals' efforts to stop or at least interrupt severe interparental conflict and/or violence. In many cases, co-parents can agree on neutralization efforts to reduce high levels of tension during pickups or drop-offs. While this is a step in the right direction, it is still a reactive measure that consumes valuable investigative time. Far too few co-parents are encouraged to take proactive steps to prevent neutralization from ever becoming necessary.

The following sections offer high-level recommendations and strategies for actively neutralizing conflict and facilitating more peaceful, harmonious relationships. These strategies support the belief that a good working relationship is the foundation for effective co-parenting. The focus is on various aspects of any co-parenting relationship that individuals can cultivate to begin finding balance with one another. This section starts with an assessment of the effectiveness of counseling and parental education services in managing conflict between multiple parents. It then provides practical advice for engaging potential or new partners in ways that enhance team spirit while discouraging potential conflicts. The section concludes with advice for handling difficult adjustments such as unemployment, homelessness, or court orders/child support.

**Attract a Supportive Community**

Even if co-parenting with a narcissist feels impossible, having a supportive community in place can be invaluable. Carry the phone numbers of your supportive friends and family members in case you need emergency support. Your community can provide emotional backing and practical assistance when things get tough.

**Utilize the Gray Rock Technique**

The **Gray Rock Technique** is designed to help you disengage from the narcissist when they use abusive tactics. By becoming unresponsive and uninterested—essentially a "gray rock"—you deprive the narcissist of the emotional reaction they seek. This technique helps you avoid being a source of narcissistic supply, thereby reducing their control over you.

**Schedule Workshops**

Until your court orders are in place, create your own schedules for logistics such as transportation, contact, and other separation-related activities. These schedules can be part of a PARR (Parenting Agreement Review and Recommendations) process, which may be necessary once you go to court. In the meantime, communicate your availability for scheduling discussions. These workshops can be conducted via messaging apps or email, but ensure they remain contained and focused.

**Responding to Tension**

Nobody has the right to treat you poorly, but narcissists often react defensively, perceiving attacks where none exist. This tension is harmful to children. When a narcissist uses conflict-adaptive behaviors such as verbal intimidation, mocking sarcasm, threats, or aggression, try using **tone reflecting** in your responses. Change the message, packaging, language, or emotional angle of your reply to address the situation indirectly or metaphorically. For example, if the narcissist sends a picture of car keys with a snide comment like, "When did you want to use these next?", you could reply with the day and time for the child's visit and conclude with, "See you Sunday!" This diffuses the situation without engaging in the intended conflict.

**Promoting Positive Communication**

At the heart of effective co-parenting is **positive communication**. This means adopting a verbal communication style that doesn't shame or minimize but instead tells the truth about your experience of separating or parallel-parenting with a narcissist. Channel negativity into exploring ways to disengage further or bolster boundaries, ensuring you remain the correct parent regardless of the narcissist's attempts to spin the truth.

**Characteristics of Positive Communication**

Parallel parenting with a narcissist involves avoiding direct discussions about the children's well-being, not attempting to undo the other parent's programming, preventing triangulation, and exchanging necessary information without delving into subjective facts or beliefs. One of the most important aspects of your "parentectomy" is to handle stress reactions positively. Ending co-parenting with a narcissist can be mired in negativity, but maintaining parallel parenting allows for potential connections and exchanges later on, especially in serious situations, without added tension. Achieving parallel parenting is essential for protecting your child and yourself from abuse that destroys self-esteem, creates deep-seated insecurities, and replaces peace with a life of tension.

# Part IV: Focusing on Raising Secure Kids

Parents often come to me as a therapist when they feel the emotional effects of co-parenting with a narcissist are impacting their children. This is a crucial topic to address. Once we have whipped our own systems and reactions to the narcissist's manipulative ways into healthy shape, we need to help our children. In many ways, this is the most integral part of the recovery process. Children should never be the crutch or primary motivator for making healthy choices regarding a narcissist; you should be. However, once you're in a healthier place, making the emotional and psychological well-being of your children a priority is essential.

In this section of *Navigating Co-Parenting with a Narcissist: A Therapeutic Guide for Creating Peace, Building Resilience, and Raising Secure Kids*, we will discuss the impact of co-parenting with a narcissist on children, including some of the root problems it creates and how it negatively affects them. We will then have a more supportive and empowering conversation about building resilience and fostering strong, healthy self-esteem in children. We will explore ways to take a "prevention" approach to help shield your kids from some harmful aspects of co-parenting with a narcissist. Additionally, we will talk about areas of empowerment for your kids—framing their experience and making them part of the solution.

**Understanding the Impact of Co-Parenting with a Narcissist on Children**

Any communication about the child seems to be an opportunity for the narcissistic parent to point out what a terrible parent you are. Your children watch and listen as one-half of their caretakers diminish in influence and experience. Your child's sense of family, love, and stable relationships is disrupted by repeated courtroom appearances and possibly CPS involvement in their life. A child raised in this dynamic becomes accustomed to having a caretaker who is an enemy and can feel that the other caretaker never really loved them, seeing how readily they participate in domination dynamics.

Narcissistic individuals often lack insight into what a child truly needs because they can't see past the limits of their own emotional inner child. Some may even leverage their child to metaphorically punch you in the gut. This can be as subtle as not saying something to the child for fear of not looking awesome or big, to outright telling the child something derogatory about you. Most children of divorced narcissists grieve a "false family" because they hold on to the ideal imagery of what should be. During that grief, it is common to blame one parent over another, a testament to the driven love they have for a family that doesn't exist.

A study of 211 U.S. undergraduates found that the impact of parental loss due to divorce is doubled when a parent has narcissistic traits. This continues into adult life, manifesting as overdeveloped addiction issues with alcohol, drugs, money, sex, and romance to fill the void left by loss. It might seem that an intact marriage between two narcissists is better for the child than a parental divorce. However, with the right data, one can rationalize a world of any truth.

**Building Resilience and Self-Esteem in Children**

Focusing on your kid's well-being is paramount.

Most narcissistic people live a life constantly trying to prove their worth. This dynamic affects the internal settings of your child when they are exposed to it. You cannot change the narcissist, but you can intervene early with your children to build strength and endurance. Resilience is the ability to bounce back from adversities. Anxiety and discomfort are natural emotions and motivators in life. Emphasize "the issue" in terms of character and strength. You are a great role model, and your children reflect your strength and perseverance.

Children who thrive are those who understand the blessing of giving. Early researchers found that children with low self-esteem received minimal encouragement from the adults in their lives or their peers and siblings. As a result, research on 2,000 middle schoolers showed that encouragement plays a significant role in their development. These are the kids who truly thrive. Their peer group's nucleus does not revolve around the need to be positive. Their nucleus is what it is—they are beyond the need to be positive. Building a strong belief system in your children and being consistent is crucial.

I never assumed I spoke for the masses, but rather for one single child with this collection of struggles. I believe change is possible for all families, especially for families of divorce. A child is not the divorce, and a family is still a family, no matter its drive for freedom and health. Your child will stand on the ground you fill with pride, love, and security, and the rest will fall to the wayside.

# Conclusion

Here we are at the end of another long journey in co-parenting with a narcissist. Whether you're at the beginning of your path or a long-time veteran of the struggle, I hope this guide has provided you with some solace and value. Bookmark it and return as often as you need. I wrote it for you because you inspired it. In this world, our boundaries are hard-earned, our work is an act of preventive maintenance, and our reward is peace. Your children learn that even when your boundaries are being crossed, you are strong, forgiving, and flexible when necessary. They learn that sometimes it's okay to let go because not everything is important, but peace and the state of our hearts and minds are. Ultimately, it is they who benefit. You can uproot and replant in any field your family's journey takes you.

Some of us have healed despite, and not because of, the narcissist. Some of us have suffered despite the added burden of their spectacular disorder. Some have had the pleasure of working through this exhausting season of our lives. The goal of this guide is to help us become the sane, mindful, and resilient individuals I've met along this journey. This reframe is about grace, growth, and the children we raise. I hope you'll benefit your children by practicing the mind-heart connection described—moving through and on because you have precious work to do. It's time to bring them an even more present, connected, and powerful you. ~ Love, Rebecca

Peace (salaam), my sisters. If only for a while, peace and blessings to all of your homes. Enacting the premise of this guide requires three key elements to counteract the effects of co-parenting with a narcissist: boundaries, peace, and raising secure children.

**Reflecting on the Journey of Co-Parenting with a Narcissist**

I was only two entries into a partnership series for Psychology Today when my attention turned completely to one particular project. As I stared into the window, reflecting on the experiences and knowledge I wanted to share, only one topic came to mind: Navigating Co-Parenting with a Narcissist. That speaks volumes! Now, sixteen entries later, it's a reflective, poignant moment to circle back and reflect on this six-part essay journey. There's nothing quite like co-parenting with a 'true narcissist.' While the term is brandished about frivolously in modern lingo, most people don't share the post-marital 'bond' that survivors of this disorder develop. While I tried to put myself in the shoes of those who lovingly Google: NPD co-parenting and secrets to kumbaya, the idealization of the NPD 'community' and lovey-dovey parenting assertions don't apply within the context of actual NPD.

The dominant pillars of this essay series reflect adaptive strategies for professionals such as psychologists, therapists, and parent-coaches—experts in families, marriage, divorce, and co-parenting. Montserrat Gas, Ph.D., brought the series to a conclusion by writing part five. Professional key takeaways nicely summarize the work we've covered so far. If you have or had an NPD ex and kids, you probably breathed a sigh and laughed at "adapting your co-parenting goals" and "choosing your battles." Dr. Fine doesn't take part in the "joys of co-parenting, one-up-parenting, or making each other's lives miserable." Rather, my words are for parents. The overall takeaway? Each of us can and should search within, heal the scars of a relationship with a narcissist.

Wondering if co-parenting with a narcissist was a good or bad thing is a pointless question. Looking at the way my ex NPD has misbehaved, I sometimes feel I never made progress. But the big picture reveals that progress isn't always fair to measure in simple terms. Growth comes from countless comeuppance moments, sometimes silly, like putting my ex NPD on advance call for important events (so I don't look surprised when they show up at my door half in tears, or when someone comes to do foreclosure proceedings). This journey has even helped me slowly make friends and understand through the perspectives of Freudian and cognitive-behavioral therapy, relating it to ninja movies and films like "The Matrix."

www.ingramcontent.com/pod-product-compliance
Lightning Source LLC
LaVergne TN
LVHW092103060526
838201LV00047B/1546